Yad b'Yad

HOLDING THE HANDS
OF JEWISH MOURNERS IN COMFORT

Dale Norma Oller, MD

LUMINARE PRESS
WWW.LUMINAREPRESS.COM

Printed in the United States of America

Cover Design by Nina Leis

Luminare Press
442 Charnelton St.
Eugene, OR 97401
www.luminarepress.com

LCCN: 2020913258
ISBN: 978-1-64388-356-4

Yad b'Yad: Holding the Hand of Mourners in Comfort
Copyright © 2017 by Dale Norma Oller, MD
First editions previously published as four pamphlets for
Congregation Neveh Shalom, Portland, Oregon

http://34blz32le6qh2cvmlktg18fr-wpengine.netdna-ssl.com/
wp-content/uploads/2018/01/Yad-B-Yad-Book-1.pdf

http://34blz32le6qh2cvmlktg18fr-wpengine.netdna-ssl.com/
wp-content/uploads/2018/01/Yad-B-Yad-Book-2.pdf

http://34blz32le6qh2cvmlktg18fr-wpengine.netdna-ssl.com/
wp-content/uploads/2018/01/Yad-B-Yad-Book-3.pdf

http://34blz32le6qh2cvmlktg18fr-wpengine.netdna-ssl.com/
wp-content/uploads/2018/01/Yad-B-Yad-Book-4.pdf

1. Jewish 2. Grief 3. Mourning Rituals

Dedicated to Rabbi Joshua (z'l) and Goldie Stampfer (z'l),
who taught me the optimism and joy of Judaism

Contents

Part 1
THE FIRST MONTH

Part 2
THE GRIEVING PROCESS

Part 3
THE MIDDLE MONTHS
OF MOURNING

Part 4
A YEAR OF MOURNING

Part 5
AFTERWORD

Foreword

Obviously, by now you know that this little gem of a book was written by Dale N. Oller, MD. I have known Dr. Oller for at least twenty-five years as a good friend and colleague.

When she told me she planned to write a book about Jewish mourning rituals, I asked myself, "Why?" Although Dr. Oller had the professional and personal expertise to write it, I wondered, "Aren't there many, too many, books on this subject? What new could be offered?" But I decided to help out by providing some of the prayers and readings from other sources for this book. After all, my forty-five-year career as an observant Jew, medical ethicist, chaplain, and social worker has been in end-of-life care and death and dying.

So, with great trepidation, I read her final draft, and boy, was I wrong. Most books about Jewish rituals of mourning are very dry and heavy. But Dr. Oller explains the psychological and emotional reasons for these rituals, such as counting the days of *shloshim*, and she weaves in her personal experiences. Who better to do this than a psychiatrist?!

This book is geared for all Jewish observers yet encourages individualism in how to practice rituals. Deference is paid to interfaith mourning, such as a Jewish adult daughter mourning her Christian father. The book provides new rituals for death due to COVID or suicide and for celebrating post-death birthdays and how to celebrate Jewish holidays in memory of your loved one. It highlights new practices of rituals, including death cafés and going to a mikvah and honoring the departed by giving the mourner an aliyah. The book explores the differences between "normal" and "complicated" grief and the warning signs to watch for. Dr. Oller pays attention to the extended family of mourners—the grandchildren, siblings, and others who are equally impacted.

Most of all, Dr. Oller weaves in her personal experience as a widow. I knew her beloved husband, Earl, for many years while he was battling multiple terminal diseases, only to keep surviving. I saw his courage and was inspired by his family's strength and love as he was dying. Actually, Earl taught all of his family and friends lessons on dying. His desire to have his family and friends show him their proposed eulogies so he could hear their loving words is described as a "new ritual" in this book.

The weaving in this book of psychological, Jewish, and personal mourning is unique. We hear and feel Dr. Oller's grief and know that, although she is a psychiatrist helping others to cope, she struggles to cope too. We are not alone in that regard. And when the world expects us to "get back to normal" after the traditional Jewish period of mourning ends, Dr. Oller says "no." Mourning continues in celebration of the loved one forever. As Dr. Oller writes, "our rituals encourage each mourner to move toward living."

Bravo and Mazel Tov, Dr. Oller! I am so glad you wrote *Yad b'Yad*.

B'Shalom
Marcia Liberson, MSW, MPH

Preface

This book is the result of my work with my synagogue, Congregation Nevah Shalom, in Portland, Oregon, following the death of my husband, Earl Oller, after forty-six years of marriage. A program called *Yad b'Yad* (Hand in Hand) was created to help other mourners appreciate the values Judaism offers in its traditional rituals around death and mourning.

Many have written about the details of these rituals. Most are rabbinic, very comprehensive, and could be overwhelming for new mourners.

This book, instead, is very personal and offers a simplified set of ideas. It emphasizes the psychological aspects of grief and mourning. As a psychiatrist with thirty years of experience, psychology is my lens, personally, with my patients, and in my community of other widows.

With intention, the quotes on the left side of this book are often short, leaving a fair amount of blank space. I encourage you to treat this book as a workbook. Jot down your own thoughts, reflections, and observations about your personal

grief and mourning process. Just as speaking (e.g., during a therapy session) moves thoughts from one place of the brain to another, writing (e.g., a journal or diary) moves thoughts in a parallel way, promoting processing. This is why many have been encouraged to keep a journal about issues or gratitude in their lives.

Unable are the loved to die. For love is immortality.

—Emily Dickinson

Dale Norma Oller, MD

PART 1

The First Month

INTRODUCTION

The purpose of this book is to offer support, comfort, and guidance as you begin to cope with the loss of a loved one. Judaism can offer a valuable roadmap to help you transition through your grief. I offer some suggestions and examples of ways to grieve.

Jewish tradition is committed to life and joy. It helps us acknowledge the sadness of loss and also provides us with rituals to mark the milestones that help us to move through the mourning process. But Judaism also mandates that in this period we move toward life and hope. Well-known psychologist Erik Erikson offers us: "Hope is the favorable ratio of basic trust over distrust." Judaism, a religion of optimism, teaches us about the power of hope.

I am standing upon the seashore. A ship at my side spreads her white sails to the morning breeze and starts for the blue ocean. She is an object of beauty and strength. I stand and watch her until at length she hangs like a speck of white cloud just where the sea and sky come to mingle with each other.

Then someone at my side says: "There, she is gone!"

"Gone where?"

Gone from my sight. That is all. She is just as large in mast and hull and spar as she was when she left my side and she is just as able to bear the load of living freight to her destined port.

Her diminished size is in me, not in her. And just at the moment when someone at my side says: "There, she is gone!" There are other eyes watching her coming, and other voices ready to take up the glad shout: "Here she comes!"

And that is dying.

—Henry Van Dyke

Dale Norma Oller, MD

Bereavement is a classic topic among psychiatrists, psychologists, and therapists. From Freud, who wrote the essay "Mourning and Melancholia" in 1917 to the present day, clinicians have developed an array of theories that touch on many aspects of this phenomenon. After thirty years of practice as one of those clinicians, I recognize that Judaism's ancient sages have offered us sound practices and rituals that, to me, are important to consider alongside these theories. Judaism and therapeutic principles, incorporated together, have created a valuable framework to help you move through the mourning process and toward life.

Darius…summoned some Greeks and asked them for how much money they would be willing to eat their dead parents. But they answered that they would not do such things for any amount of money. And after that Darius summoned some Indians (called Kallatiai), who eat their parents, and asked them for what price they would agree to burn their dead fathers with fire. But they shouted aloud and bid him not to speak blasphemy. Thus these things are established by custom and quite right was Pindar, it seems to me, when he says in a poem custom is king of all.

—Herodotus (trans. Anne Carson)

Customs

Different cultures and religions have customs that strongly contribute to rituals regarding death, bereavement, and grief. Many would offend our current sensibilities, yet current Jewish rituals seem as sound today as they did in ancient times.

The Three S's:
Shomrim, Shiva, and *Shloshim*

Shomrim:

Shomer, the Hebrew word for "guardian," is part of our 2000-year-old Jewish tradition to honor the dead. We do not want to leave our loved ones alone from the time of death until burial. The shomer, either a family member or a dear friend, will watch over the body until the funeral begins. The shomer might recite psalms or other religious texts. This sweet tradition of guarding the body is the beginning of the soul's ascent on its journey to heaven.

This concept was not new to me. For thirty-five years I have volunteered in the *Chevra Kaddisha* ("Holy Committee" or Burial Society). We perform taharah—we prepare Jews for their casket in a tender, traditional purification ceremony. As part of the Chevra, we sit with the body until it is taken to the cemetery. Frequently I did not know the person in the casket but, nonetheless, I have performed this loving act with serious and honorable attention to what our tradition prescribes.

However, it was not until my husband's death that I appreciated the power of this time-honored Jewish tradition. When asking our family and

I Recall

In memory of lives that touched one's own

I call her/him to mind and heart,
the texture of his/her life,
its presence in mine.

Images rise up
and fall away,
moments in the current of time—

tender, harsh,
extraordinary,
mundane,
that which gives pleasure in recollection
and that which hurts, yet resists
being forgotten.

May the threads of memory be woven
into the fabric of my life
and bring healing.

—Marcia Falk

friends to participate as shomrim for him, I was so
pleased that everyone who was asked was indeed
willing to sit with him at the funeral home. Waiting for the Sabbath to end required some to spend
hours at night with him and others to arrive at
early morning shifts around the clock. The feed-
back I received from all who participated was
astounding! They shared what a positive experience it was for them. It provided a time to reflect
on their relationship with my husband. It was
a time to cry, to smile, and to recall their lives
together. It was a time to think about their own
mortality. No doubt, there were those who chose
not to read psalms but instead chose to talk with
my husband's body. I thought that was perfectly
acceptable and what my husband would have
wanted. Over and over, I was thanked for such a
meaningful mitzvah opportunity.

Two months later, when I became a shomer
for my aunt, I felt the sacredness of this ritual even
more deeply. This act of lovingkindness following a
death was gratifying. Knowing that this lovely role
was a way to help the soul of a loved one reach the
Garden of Eden was indeed very satisfying.

Rabbi David Kosak of Congregation Nevah
Shalom wrote on one Shabbat about the concept of
a "doula of the soul." When the doulas are friends

The Lord is my shepherd; I shall not want. He makes me lie down in green pastures; He leads me beside the still waters.
He restores my soul; He leads me on the paths of righteousness for His name's sake.

Yea, though I walk through the valley of the shadow of death, I shall fear no evil,
for Thou art with me;
Thy rod and thy staff, they comfort me.

You prepare a table for me in the presence of my enemies: You anoint my head with oil; my cup runneth over.
Surely goodness and mercy shall follow me all the days of my life:
And I will dwell in the house of the Lord forever.

—Psalm 23

and family, theirs is a heightened connection in performing this mitzvah. It can be a meaningful experience, a comfort to the mourners, and a personal way of understanding our tradition's valuable lessons.

I encourage you to consider the powerfully positive experience in trying to arrange for shomrim.

Shiva:

Shiva is a familiar word to most of us. It means "seven," which relates to the first seven days of mourning after the burial of a first-degree relative. The term "sitting shiva" comes from the low, uncomfortable benches that some communities provide for the mourners in their home following a death. The minyan (ten people present) in the home can be beneficial for the mourning family. It is an opportunity to say the Mourner's Kaddish (a prayer for the dead) with a communal presence. It is an opportunity to stay within the home for the first week following a death. It is an opportunity to talk further about the person who has just died. Sweet stories, remembrances, and further focus following the more formal funeral help honor this loved one. Grandchildren might get to know their beloved grandparent better through these

*Worship is a way of seeing the world
in the light of God.*

—Rabbi Abraham Joshua Heschel

stories. Friends offer memories that may make the mourners smile. The informality is psychologically helpful after both the strained wait for the funeral and the burial.

The mourners are not hosts to those attending shiva minyanim. Friends provide a meal of condolence and physically serve the mourners. Some mourners of the family wear slippers. After all, it is a week of mourning and of staying within the immediate family home.

You may choose to have one shiva minyan, multiple minyanim, or none at all: it is completely up to the family. Our busy lives are often scheduled with nighttime meetings, classes, and activities. By choosing to hold several nights of shiva minyanim, it allows all friends and relatives to participate in one or more of these gatherings.

It is a mitzvah to comfort mourners. For many mourners, this might be their first experience with this process and at a time when they are feeling the most vulnerable. There is a tradition that I found quite meaningful: at the end of the seven days of shiva, the first leaving of the home is often a walk around the block. It is the first entrance into the world again.

Multiple nightly minyanim are exhausting, even if food preparation and clean-up is man-

There is a time and a season
For every desire beneath heaven.

There is a time to be born
And a time to die;
A time to plant, and a time to uproot.
There is a time to kill and a time to heal;
A time to cry and a time to laugh,
A time to eulogize and a time to dance.
A time to throw stones
*   and a time to gather stones;*

A time to embrace, and a time to refrain.
A time to seek and a time to lose.
A time to keep and a time to discard.
A time to rend, and a time to sew.
A time for silence, and a time for speech.

—Ecclesiastes (Kohelet 3:1-7)

Dale Norma Oller, MD

aged by others. However, the purpose of shiva is clear—to surround the mourners with community. Like the "Wings of *Shekhinah*," a reference to the feminine God, the shiva ritual lifts you out of bed each day and wraps you protectively like a tallit (a prayer shawl) around your shoulders. It is this support and warmth of being surrounded by relatives and friends that will help you move toward living again. This is the basis of all Jewish traditions of death and mourning.

I encourage you to ask for help with the shiva minyamin. You may be physically and emotionally exhausted, therefore this is a time to rely on your community.

After my husband, Earl, died, my friends and relatives took time out of their lives to be with my family. They told stories and shared memories, some of which I had never heard before! Months later, I grasped the power of this ancient tradition. I began to trust the wisdom of Judaism's rituals as a comfort at this time of shock and loss. When it is difficult to truly know what to do, the formula is spelled out for us. We are completely free to participate in any, all, or none of these prescribed rituals.

There are stars whose light only reaches the earth long after they have fallen apart. There are people whose remembrance gives light in this world, long after they have passed away. This light shines in our darkest nights on the road we must follow.

—The Talmud

Shloshim:

The word *shloshim* means thirty. In this case, it refers to the thirty days following burial, and it includes the shiva week. Judaism wisely helps the mourner along the journey of intense grief and shock to living again by marking periods of time. One could say that the sages of long ago were much like the present-day psychologist treating grief. Marking periods of time with gradual return to living is psychologically sound. Counting is a frequent theme in Jewish practice. We count the Omer, days between Passover and Shavuot holidays. We count the days of a week until Shabbat. We count the nights of Hanukkah. Counting the thirty days of shloshim takes on a rhythm of its own after a loss. It gives us structure—a beginning and an end.

When someone has lost a spouse, child, or sibling, it is Jewish tradition to recite the Mourner's Kaddish for thirty days. This is different than the loss of a parent, when the Mourner's Kaddish is to be said for approximately a year (eleven months and one day). As with all of the prescribed traditions, I encourage you to do what feels best. If saying the Mourner's Kaddish for a spouse for the year is preferred, the mourner is certainly welcome

Mourner's Kaddish

Let God's Name be made great and holy in the world that was created as God willed. May God complete the holy realm in your lifetime, in your days, and in the days of all the house of Israel, quickly and soon. And say: Amen.

May God's great Name be blessed, forever and as long as worlds endure.

May it be blessed, and praised, and glorified, and held in honor, viewed with awe, embellished, and revered; and may the Blessed Name of Holiness be hailed, though it be higher than all the blessings, songs, praises, and consolations that we utter in this world. And say: Amen.

May Heaven grant a universal peace, and life for us, and for all Israel. And say: Amen.

May the One who created harmony above, make peace for us and for all Israel, and for all who dwell on earth. And say: Amen.

Dale Norma Oller, MD

to do so. If attending morning minyan every day for thirty consecutive days is helpful, the "morning minyaneers" are delighted and welcoming. If attending morning minyan on a particular day of the week (i.e., every Tuesday) is the personal commitment, this, too, provides rhythm.

Attending morning minyan may be a completely new experience and, thus, one that is intimidating. The morning minyan "regulars" at my synagogue were a warm, friendly group. They are completely non-judgmental of your familiarity—or lack thereof—with the service. They were delighted that I joined them. On some mornings, you may make that tenth person to be a "minyan," which will permit the saying of communal prayers. Morning "minyaneers" are there each morning for each of their own reason. One reason is to create ten people to comfort you communally. They say a loud "Amen" during the segments of the Mourner's Kaddish, an auditory comfort and a message that is to convey "we are sorry for your loss." I looked forward to their welcoming smiles, greetings of "good morning," playfulness, and, of course, their reliable presence permitted me to say the Mourner's Kaddish each morning of shloshim. Their presence was an unexpected gift at a time when I felt vulnerable.

Grieve not,
Nor speak of me with tears,
But laugh and talk of me
As if I were beside you.
I loved you so—
'twas Heaven here with you.

—Isla Paschal Richardson

Also inherent in shloshim is a time for tzedakah. Inaccurately translated as "charity," it literally means righteousness or justice. It is a time to think about donating to organizations or causes that the person who died is now unable to donate to.

After my husband's death, I created my own rhythm of shloshim that felt very satisfying and was a poignant way to mark the thirty days. Attending minyan each morning, I returned home and wrote a check to a different organization for each of the thirty days. It was a way to combine both saying the Mourner's Kaddish and fulfilling the mitzvah of tzedakah. After years of practicing psychiatry, I knew at some level there were two important aspects of moving along in the grieving process that could be accomplished by the rhythm of shloshim: 1) creating a personal ritual and 2) marking time in a thoughtful way. I chose with intention the amount of $18 to gift each of the thirty organizations. The gematria is an alpha-numeric code of assigning a numerical value to a name, word, or phrase based on its letters. The number eighteen is CHAI, meaning LIFE. How fitting to think about LIFE as I plodded through the first thirty days after DEATH.

Even if you are not a morning person and 7:15 a.m. is not your best time of day, I highly recommend you try saying the Mourner's Kaddish at a

Not to have had pain is not to have been human.

—Yiddish proverb

Dale Norma Oller, MD

morning minyan for the comforting experience it may provide. In my case, since it was the loss of a spouse, after shloshim, I was permitted to be given an aliyah (called to the Torah). Torah services occur on Mondays, Thursdays, and Saturdays at my synagogue. It was a powerful moment to be able to mark the end of shloshim, touching the Torah with my tallit, saying the prayer before and after the Torah reading. All of the rituals in Judaism have a specific purpose, and this marks the time to move on to the next stage of grieving, which was, for me, to go back to work. I thanked the friendly morning minyan "regulars" for the help and love with which they surrounded me. I even committed to being a once-a-week "regular" myself!

My Hebrew skills are modest, but the morning minyan "regulars" never seemed to mind if during the Amidah (silent prayer), I simply closed my eyes and did my own meditation, which brought me calmness. Some prayers are chanted too quickly for me to follow along, so I used that time to again close my eyes and smile at my memories. The stained glass windows in the small chapel at my synagogue are of the exact colors of the impatiens that my husband planted each year. They, too, caught my attention each morning, and I vowed to plant his flowers in the early summer.

*It is not enough to recognize your conflicting emotions; you must deal with them openly. That is why there is a mourning period. This is a time to share your feelings. An emotion that is denied expression is **not** destroyed. You only prolong the agony and delay the grief process.*

—Dr. Earl A. Grollman

Morning minyan can be a very personal time to reflect on what has happened in your life. It is a place that encourages mindfulness. All of this in a short half hour early each morning is a way to begin another day that can still feel unreal, painful, and even "unbelievable."

But Achilles went on grieving for his friend, whom he could not banish from his mind, and all-conquering sleep refused to visit him. He tossed to one side and the other, thinking always of his loss of Patrochus's manliness and spirit... of fights with the enemy and adventures on unfriendly seas. As memories crowded in on him, the warm tears poured down his cheeks.

—Homer, *The Iliad*

PART 2

The Grieving Process

INTRODUCTION

The purpose of this part of the book is to offer you support, comfort, and guidance as you continue to cope with the loss of your loved one. This part of the book focuses on the grieving process itself.

Grieving is a process, and it cannot be rushed. It is not linear, and each day can be different. There is neither a right nor wrong way to grieve. It is exhausting and stressful. Each loss is unique, and thus, one cannot compare the processes. Some mourn through tears, some through telling the story, and some through prayer and ritual. Some mourn in silence and some with words.

Grief is intense. Initially, it is a combination of trauma and separation. It can appear as a "painful protest," a struggle to accept, or a yearning and

No one ever told me that grief felt so like fear.

—C. S. Lewis, in *A Grief Observed*

longing for the lost loved one. Sometimes there are strong thoughts to reminisce or even a wish "to be with" a loved one. This is all normal. Each person has his/her own path as well as a timeline of experiencing the grief process.

Normal Grieving

Grief can manifest itself in emotional, physical, and cognitive changes. First, emotions can be intense and varied. They can be a mixture of sadness, remorse, guilt, anger, fear, and even relief. Emotional symptoms vary from individual to individual. It is common to feel flat, apathetic, uninterested, disconnected, and irritable.

Second, it is not uncommon to experience physical/bodily responses, including change in appetite, digestive symptoms, dry mouth, sleep disturbances, fatigue/exhaustion, restlessness, and uncontrollable sighing. Similar to fear, grief is a stress reaction. The immune and hormonal systems are vulnerable. It is stressful to support a loved one through treatment and the dying process. It is also stressful to experience the shock of a sudden death. I would advise a visit to your doctor if your symptoms seem exaggerated. An angry thyroid gland might go on strike from its

Weep not in excess for the dead, neither bemoan him too much.

—Jeremiah 22:10

connection to the stress hormone, cortisol. Lab tests are a good idea. It is a particularly important time to take care of your physical health.

Third, grieving has been known to cause cognitive symptoms. Difficulty with attention, focus, and memory are common. For many, a typical response begins with an "emotional fog."

Brother Toby, from the Starcross Monastic Community, offers the following concept: "Words can be powerful. For some, 'sadness' seems too weak. For some, 'grief' seems too dark. 'Loss' connotes something that might well be found. What we may truly want to say is that we want to feel his or her hand just once more."

For the last thirty years, I have worked with grieving patients. My training was steeped in concepts of "bereavement," "grief," and "mourning" of losses. However, until I lost my own husband, the descriptive words blended and overlapped but did not always resonate. Definitions may serve to help distinguish these "normal" responses after a loss of a loved one. Bereavement is the reaction to death. Grief is the emotional and/or psychological reaction to loss but not limited to death. Mourning is the social expression of bereavement or grief that is formalized by culture, custom, and/or religion.

The numbing agony after losing your spouse is so overwhelming. It is so devastating. I still feel shredded. It is my wish that reading this will be of benefit to other women and men who have gone through the long, dark pathway of loss. My purpose and hope is that there will be points of identification that will click and be of comfort. Each of us has our own story.

—Katey Geyer Winant,
One Washcloth, One Towel, 2011

A colleague of mine gave me a small tender book with the title *One Washcloth, One Towel* after my husband, Earl, died. I resonated with the words. However, the illustrations pierced my very being. The initial illustration showed a bathroom towel rod with two wash cloths and two towels. A subsequent illustration showed the same bathroom rod with one washcloth and one towel. For me the latter illustration spoke volumes and continues to be a reminder. This symbolism became my reality. It was more powerful than seeing his closet with his clothes, his tie rack, or his shoes. These items are very hard for many to remove from the home. Even removing a spouse's toothbrush can be wrenching. Widows tell me this all the time.

Emptiness has a loud sound. It is an incessant drone, like whispers we can't make out or the sound of water draining out of the tub. I want to thrash around and get away from it. But it follows me. Everywhere, it follows me. And when there are sounds of life around me, they grate against my wounds, amplifying my own inner emptiness—the aloneness I did not choose.

There is only one thing to do. Be still. The silence will eventually become a friend. And within it, maybe we can hear what we've never heard before.

—Stephanie Ericsson,
Companion Through the Darkness, 1993

COMPLICATED GRIEF

Grief is painful. Everyone who grieves can use a helping hand and a listening ear. But how do you know if you would benefit from extra help from an expert in loss and bereavement issues? What clues might indicate you could use professional care?

Below are two lists to help you decide if you are among the 10 percent of those experiencing "complicated/prolonged grief" or "clinical depression." Any grieving person might experience these briefly. However, if you sense your symptoms are exaggerated, it may benefit you to seek professional help, if only to reassure yourself that you're on the right path.

The Hospice Foundation of America offers ten questions about various aspects of grief.

1. Are you *always* irritable, annoyed, intolerant, or angry these days?

2. Do you experience an *ongoing* sense of numbness or of being isolated from yourself or from others? Do you usually feel that you have no one to talk to about what's happened?

*The capacity to be consoled is a
consequential distinction between grief
and depression.*

—Kay Jamison, MD

Dale Norma Oller, MD

3. Since your loved one died are you *highly* anxious *most* of the time about your own death or the death of someone you love? Is it beginning to interfere with your relationships, your ability to concentrate, or life as you would like to live it?

4. Do you feel that you are *always* and *continually* preoccupied with your loved one, his or her death, or certain aspects of it even though it's been several months since his or her death?

5. Do you *usually* feel restless or in "high gear"? Do you feel the need to be constantly busy...beyond what's normal for you?

6. Are you afraid of becoming close to new people for fear of losing again?

7. Do you find yourself acting in ways that might prove harmful to you over time: drinking more than you used to; using more prescription or non-prescription drugs; engaging in sexual activity that is unsafe or unwise; driving in an unsafe or reckless manner (beyond what's normal for you), or entertaining serious thoughts about suicide?

A Prayer When a Loved One Dies After a Long and Painful Illness

I miss you. I am lonely without you. I am devastated that you were taken from me. I am angry that you had to suffer so. It was so hard to see you in your torment and pain. But that's not how I will remember you.

I will always remember you full of life and warmth and kindness. I will remember the laughter and the love. I will remember the precious time we shared. I will remember your vitality and your grace.

Your death has left a gaping hole in my life. But as hard as it is to be without you, I take comfort in the knowledge that you are at last at peace and free of pain.

Rest in peace. God bless you. Amen.

—Rabbi Naomi Levy

Dale Norma Oller, MD

8. Are you taking on too much responsibility for surviving family members or close friends? What's too much responsibility? That varies greatly and depends on the situation, but if you're feeling heavily burdened by it, angry, or like the situation is "suffocating" you, it might be time to speak with someone.

9. Do your grief reactions continue *over time* to be limited in some way? Are you experiencing only a few of the reactions or emotions that usually come with grief? Are you unable to express your thoughts or feelings about your loved one and his or her death in words or in actions? Do you remember only certain aspects of your loved one or of your relationship together. For example, are you recalling only the good parts as opposed to a more complete and balanced view of him or her?

10. Is there some aspect of what you're experiencing that makes you wonder about whether you're normal or going crazy? Do you feel stuck in your grief in some way, unable to move forward, even though it has been quite some time since your loved one's death?

*Who shares in the community's trouble
will also share in its consolation.*

—Babylonian Talmud

Dale Norma Oller, MD

Copied with permission from the Hospice Foundation of America, Dr. Charles F. Reynolds III, et al, offers an additional list of complicated grief symptoms in his 2011 book titled *Diagnoses and Treatment of Complicated Grief*:

1. Preoccupation with the person who died

2. Memories of the person who died are upsetting

3. The death is unacceptable

4. Longing for the person who died

5. Drawn to places and things associated with the person who died

6. Anger about the death

7. Disbelief

8. Feeling stunned or dazed

9. Difficulty trusting others

10. Difficulty caring about others

11. Avoidance of reminders of the person who died

12. Pain in the same area of the body

O God of my deliverance,
When I cry out in the night before You,
Let my prayer reach You.
Incline Your ear to my cry...
O God, I am like one who
has lost all strength,
Wandering freely among
the dead.

—Psalm 88

Dale Norma Oller, MD

13. Feeling that life is empty

14. Hearing the voice of the person who died

15. Seeing the person who died

16. Feeling it is unfair to live when the other person has died

17. Bitter about the death

18. Envious of others

19. Lonely

While Judaism clearly marks the time during the first month, the subsequent months of grieving are more fluid and individualized. Rituals encourage each mourner to move toward living.

Searching for Shalom

I see your pain and want to banish it with the wave of a star, but have no star.

I see your tears and want to dry them with the hem of an angel's gown, but have no angel.

I see your heart fallen to the ground and want to return it wrapped in cloths woven of rainbow, but have no rainbow.

God is the One who has stars and angels and rainbows, and we are the ones God sends to sit beside you until the stars come out and the angels dry your tears and your heart is back in place, rainbow-blessed.

—Ann Weems

Forgotten Groups of Mourners

You may be a part of a group of mourners not often addressed in our traditions. For example, a grandchild who lost a beloved grandparent may choose to stand and say the Mourner's Kaddish. A spouse or sibling may choose to say the Mourner's Kaddish for the year rather than the prescribed month of shloshim.

Additionally, grandparents are a forgotten set of profound mourners. Losing a grandchild can be an especially devastating loss because it is "out of generational order." Bereaved grandparents have more life experience with death, and therefore, our culture expects them to cope on their own.

PART 3

The Middle Months of Mourning

INTRODUCTION

The purpose of this part of the book is to focus on the middle months of mourning. These are months with fewer prescribed rituals. Many mourners have found creative ways to bridge the gap between the first and last months of traditional observances of mourning.

Shomrim, shiva, and shloshim, the"3 S's," offer practical guidance during the first month of mourning. These practices have been passed down through the generations. Similarly, the end of the mourning period is ritually prescribed, and includes an unveiling and yahrzeit, the Hebrew calendar anniversary of someone's death.

I have thought about why Judaism omits middle

A Prayer for the Comfort of Memory

God, what I fear most is forgetting him. I've already lost his presence in my life, I can't bear the thought of losing his presence in my mind, my heart, and my soul.

I want to remember it all. His touch, his smell, the look in his eyes. Our conversations, our silences, even our disagreements. I want to remember him as he was without turning him into some kind of saint. I loved him in all his complexity, in all his imperfection.

Help me to remember, God. As I make my way through my busy and sometimes lonely days, may thoughts of him lead me back to times of smiles and laughter. Let my tears and pain be eased by the comfort of his memory.

I will carry the lessons he taught me always. I will try my best to live up to the example he set for me.

Send me strength, God, and comfort, now and always. Amen.

—Rabbi Naomi Levy, *Talking To God*, 2002

month rituals, other than Yizkor. Yizkor is the opening word of the memorial prayers recited four times a year. Our religion is known to have come from sophisticated and psychologically-minded sages. The sages must have known about the protective nature of an "emotional fog" that many experience during these middle months. For some, that translates into moving through space and time clouded by a numbing, sleepy, unfocused existence. Others may experience this time as a frantic, busy, distracted existence. Each mourner has his/her own tempo and style. There is no "normal" way to mourn. Perhaps the sages intentionally left this period of time for your own creation.

CREATIVE RITUALS

Creating a ritual is a powerful way for individuals, family, and friends to remember. It must be YOUR ritual, for if others suggest one, it is their ritual for you to follow. Given the paucity of rituals during this lengthy "middle period" of mourning, I offer ideas and encouragement to be creative and develop your own respectful, appropriate, and meaningful observances.

Following shloshim, Earl's beloved garden began to bud and bloom. Gardening was his pas-

A Litany of Remembrance

At the rising of the sun and at its going down,
we remember them.
At the blowing of the wind and in the chill of
winter,
we remember them.
At the opening of the buds and in the rebirth
of spring,
we remember them.
At the blueness of the skies and in the warmth
of summer,
we remember them.
At the rustling of the leaves and in the beauty
of autumn,
we remember them.
At the beginning of the year and when it ends,
we remember them.
As long as we live, they too will live, for they are
now a part of us as,
we remember them.
When we are weary and in need of strength,
we remember them.
When we are lost and sick at heart,
we remember them.
When we have joy we crave to share,
we remember them.

sion, and it promoted his equanimity. I discovered that bringing his beautiful flowers into the house and using the empty memorial candle container as a vase gave me comfort.

A second ritual developed during the preparation to sell the family home. This house was our gathering place for every Shabbat dinner and every holiday. Therefore, I asked my adult children and grandchildren to gather and walk around every corner of the house, to quietly say goodbye to the dwelling that was filled with Earl's memories and collections. This could be a private, sweet, tearful, and meaningful ritual for any family, whether staying or leaving the home.

Another ceremony developed when I invited Earl's close cousins and our family to transplant a few of his roses. He would have been delighted knowing that his roses are now growing in the yards of his loved ones. This activity bridged the gap of time between shloshim and yahrzeit. It is not a coincidence that I chose a rose for the cover of this book.

We created yet another new ritual that would have been important to Earl. Tradition suggests that we leave a stone rather than cut flowers on Jewish gravesites. We, however, transplanted Earl's rose bushes on his grave and interspersed them with stones.

When we have decisions that are difficult to make,
we remember them.
When we have achievements that are based on theirs,
we remember them.
As long as we live, they too will live, for they are now a part of us as we remember them.

—Rabbi Sylvan Kamens and
Rabbi Jack Riemer

Placing stones is not exclusive to Jewish graves and not a strict Jewish tradition. For thousands of years, people were buried into the earth at the spot where they died. Rocks and stones on top of shallow graves kept animals from digging up bodies. Also, early Eastern European folklore feared the dead body's spirit could escape and torment others. Today, the stone indicates the grave was visited and the person remembered. Stones are strong and lasting whereas flowers wilt.

Candles are significant to us as Jews. The memorial candle burns for seven days starting after the funeral through shiva. The yahrzeit candle burns for twenty-four hours to remember the anniversary of the death of our loved one. The Shabbat candles have a certain number of hours to burn. We burn candles at Hanukkah. Candles have a beginning and an end. They undergo a change of state—melting to wax. Mourners are also undergoing a change of state. Perhaps you would like to incorporate a candle in your new ritual.

Birthday Poem for My Grandmother
for L.B.M.C., 1890-1975

I stood on the porch tonight—which way do we
face to talk to the dead? I thought of the new rose,
and went out over the
grey lawn—things really
have no color at night. I descended
the stone steps, as if to the place where one
speaks to the dead. The rose stood
half-uncurled, glowing white in the
black air. Later I remembered
your birthday.

You would have been ninety and getting
roses from me. Are the dead there
if we do not speak to them? When I came to see you
you were always sitting quietly in the chair,
not knitting, because of the arthritis,
not reading, because of the blindness,
just sitting. I never knew how you
did it or what you were thinking. Now I
sometimes sit on the porch, waiting,
trying to feel you there like the color of the
flowers in the dark.

—Sharon Olds,
The Dead and the Living, 1992

Jewish Holidays throughout the Year

Important Jewish holidays and festivals occur throughout the first year of mourning. Rabbi Kerry Olitzky offers ideas on ways that the holidays can impact mourners. The Days of Awe or High Holidays often present an especially poignant emptiness without your loved one. Sitting in synagogue for hours on Rosh Hashanah can be painful. The sound of the shofar (ram's horn) may jolt you back to the sound of filling the grave with dirt. The Yom Kippur Yizkor service is a powerfully reflective time. The focus on who will live and who will die is unavoidably reminiscent of your loved one who has died. Sukkot is a time to think about the fragility of life, a theme mourners are all too aware of. Hanukkah is a holiday that celebrates miracles during a threatening period in Jewish history. Mourning, for many, can be a time of threatened faith. To watch others celebrate the joyous holiday of Purim can be a temporary relief from the pain of mourning. Elijah's empty chair at the Passover Seder table is all too symbolic of the empty chair of our lost loved one. And finally, Shavuot is our spring holiday. For those in mourning, perhaps it symbolizes the painful "winter" of

Birthday Poem

The last movie we saw with you has been
nominated for an award—
You're not here to say I told you so.
The retractable back scratcher and chocolate bar
we were going to bring to you,
gifts picked up in the drugstore checkout line,
rest on the table by the door, getting dusty.
We talk of the things you tended on the earth.
The barbecue, the deck, the grape arbors
and the rain barrels to feed them,
the sprouts growing in the greenhouse.
The trail, the coastlines,
the crooked roads you led us down.
The big unfettered sound of your amusement.
Slowly, we begin to see the story in the black-and-
white photographs:
The worried child you always were,
Your knit brows and hopeful smile as if asking,
Is everything all right?
Did I do something wrong?
You were supposed to get better.
We baked a cake for you
And we brought it to the place you loved
and scattered the pieces like ashes.
It was your birthday without you.

—Sally Charette

loss that is followed by the "blossoming spring" of going forward with life.

Birthdays, Anniversaries, and Other "Hallmark" Celebrations

The anticipation of the "first" of any significant holiday without your loved one can be distressing. Marking these dates by creating a new ritual might be helpful.

There are no Jewish traditions for how to celebrate the birthday of a loved one who has died. Now you are faced with the dilemma of how to mark this important date without your loved one.

My patients have taught me over the past thirty years of clinical practice in psychiatry that continuing to honor each birthday of a departed loved one is powerfully important. Whether it is a parent, spouse or child, a special friend or relative, birthdays are never forgotten, just as death dates are never forgotten.

Judaism's focus is on death dates, as opposed to our American culture's focus on birth dates. Only one reference to birthdays is found in the Bible—Pharaoh's. The Mishnah points out that birthdays are considered solemn days, a reminder that one is moving closer to the end of life.

Mourner's Kaddish

May God's great Name be extolled and hallowed throughout the world.

And may God's kingdom be established in our lives and days and the lives of all of the House of Israel speedily in approaching times. Amen.

May God's great Name be praised forever and ever.

Blessed and praised and heightened, carried and glorified, raised and chanted is the Name of the Holy Blessed One who is above all blessings and praises. Our guide and comforter, redeemer for all eternity. Amen.

May a great peace descend from the heavens upon all who live, and upon the house of Israel and let us say: Amen.

May the One who makes peace in the high places bring peace upon us and all of Israel, and let us say: Amen.

As Jews, we can borrow from our American culture's traditions. My dear friend Brenda died several years ago of ovarian cancer. Every year on her birthday, her friends and relatives gather for a meal and a time to remember her. Some read a poem that reminds them of Brenda. Some tell a sweet story of an experience with her. Some use the gathering to remember a trait or virtue of Brenda and then reflect on how that trait has made an impact on their own life. This has been a meaningful way for Brenda's circle of friends to keep her alive.

The loss of a spouse presents another poignant date to remember—the wedding anniversary. "We would have been married __ years!" is a common statement. Again, I urge you to find your own ritual for this significant date. Private or with others, it is not helpful to try to ignore it—it is nearly impossible.

CREATIVITY

Our congregation is welcoming to many styles of practicing Judaism. Using the rituals that Judaism so wisely provides us does not prohibit us from being creative. Many congregants are part of interfaith marriages and families. One congregant, Sandy Axel, shares below her interfaith experience of mourning her father:

For those of us who have chosen Judaism as our spiritual home, the process of mourning for a loved one can be complicated. How do we honor the one who has passed and the traditions of our birth family while staying true to ourselves and the faith we have embraced as adults?

Creativity and sensitivity to our family's needs and our own can help guide our mourning process. When my father died, our family worked together to create observances that were meaningful for all of us. A devout Catholic, my father attended Mass weekly; how would I honor this devotion but stay true to myself?

We had a funeral service for Dad at the funeral home, which followed the Catholic rite, but at the cemetery I said Kaddish at his graveside. We had shiva minyan AND a wake, which satisfied both my needs and the needs of my family. I recited the

Yizkor for one well-loved:

You,_____, were my _____. I remember you now, my beloved, my friend. I recall the days of love, companionship, and happiness we shared and the trials we overcame. Although we are parted now, the bond that unites our souls can never be severed. You live now and always within my heart, and you sweeten my life. I have contributed tzedakah in your memory to perpetuate the goodness which you brought to this world. May the Infinite, which has claimed you, bless you and keep you and grant you eternal peace, Amen.

Mourner's Kaddish for eleven months. And on the anniversary of his death, my sisters and mother gathered from around the country to remember him—I went to minyan to recite the Mourner's Kaddish once again (but did not recite El Malei Rachamin*), and then we all went to the cemetery to put flowers on his grave. We then went to a Catholic shrine to light a candle for him, and once we returned home, I lit a yahrzeit candle too.*

This is the pattern I will follow each year on the anniversary of his passing to honor and remember him and to stay true to this life I have chosen for myself.

Yizkor

The ritual that Judaism does offer us, not only during the middle months of grieving but also throughout each year, is Yizkor. Yizkor, which is Hebrew for "remember," is a memorial service that takes place four times a year: 1) the last day of Passover, 2) the second day of Shavuot, 3) on Shemini Atzeret, and 4) on Yom Kippur. For many Jews, this word is familiar as part of the Yom Kippur liturgy. Yet for many, the knowledge that it is also said three other times during the calendar year is often not known.

Yizkor for one who may
also have been a source of pain or
difficulty:

*You, _____, were my _____. My memories
of you are both painful and pleasant. I can neither fully embrace nor fully negate the love I feel
for you. I can fully acknowledge the many effects
you had on my life and the lessons I learned in
our relationship while you were alive and since
your death. I have contributed tzedakah in
your memory. I pray for increasing resolution
in our connection and increasing peacefulness
for your spirit.*

Yizkor is based on the belief of the eternity of the soul. Therefore it is traditional to give tzedakah in honor of the loved one who has died. This is a deed that the loved one can no longer do him/herself. Another tradition is to light a Yizkor candle, which burns for twenty-four hours.

The first Yizkor service of the year of mourning could be experienced in a completely different state of emotions from the second, third, or fourth. It could open floodgates of tears. Yizkor can be a time for personal healing and growth. As we recite the Mourner's Kaddish together with Jews all over the world, we remember that death is an inevitable part of life. We mourn those who died before their time, those who died in suffering and pain, those whose lives enriched the world, and we remember the living. Saying the Mourner's Kaddish is not a prayer that praises the dead. Rather, it is a prayer that praises God and the power of God in the world.

Another emotional day in my experience was on the second day of Shavuot. Across the country, many congregations, including mine, use this date to purchase a memorial plaque for the synagogue. Was it the harshness of metal? Was it the first time to see the death date under my husband's name stamped into a permanent marker? Or was

They still live on earth in the acts of goodness they performed, and in the hearts of those who cherish their memory.

—Reform Jewish Union Prayer Book

Dale Norma Oller, MD

it because it followed yet another Yizkor service? It was hard to sort out at the time of this writing, but again, I urge you to have that relative or friend with you for support. It can be a powerful short service.

Mourning is Individual

Not all of us mourn using prayer. For some, nature is the best vehicle of comfort. For some, tzedakah comforts and is part of our tradition. For some, finding volunteerism and "mitzvah opportunities" bring the most comfort. Mourning is such an individual process. There is clearly no right or wrong way to journey through mourning and grief.

For me, smiling at a photo of my husband every morning starts my day thinking about him, and it has become a daily practice and one that comforts. It fits nicely with a little mantra of Modah Ani, equanimity. It rhymes and is simple. It serves me to thank God for letting me wake every morning, and it serves to remind me of my husband's strongest "soul trait"—equanimity. This daily prayer grounds me for the difficulties I experience going through routine life after his death.

Death Café

One activity, though certainly not for everyone, that intrigued me was attending a couple of death café meetings. Among my large circle of friends, there were not many I would even think to ask to accompany me. However, my cousin, Charlene Zidell, and her mother, my Aunt Min, were always comfortable talking about death. They financially supported Governor Barbara Roberts of Oregon with the second edition of a book about her husband, Frank, and the Roberts' quest for "death with dignity."

The venue was Portland's long-standing Clinton Street Theatre. Somehow, I had never gone there for their famous run at midnight of *The Rocky Horror Picture Show*. I was always more comfortable with death than horror.

Participants ranged from hospice personnel to Hemlock Society advocates to "death with dignity" proponents. Additionally, people like myself facing a family member's death might be in attendance. Full-length movies, shorts, and group discussions led by moderators were what I observed. This international organization could be of interest to some who are in the throes of anticipatory grief or other times along this grieving process.

A Prayer When a Parent Dies

I miss you. You gave me my life. You were my protector, my teacher, my moral compass, my comfort. I feel so alone without you. No one worries about me the way you did. No one loves me the way you did.

Please forgive me for the times I caused you pain, and for the times I took you for granted. I can't begin to fathom all the sacrifices you made for my sake.

I want to thank you for all the ways you blessed my life. Nothing can replace the gaping hole your death has left in my life. But mixed together with all my sadness, there is a great joy for having known you.

I will remember your smile, your touch. I will remember your laughter, your kindness, your generosity, your determination, your love.

Thank you for the time we shared, for the love you gave, for the wisdom you spread. I will always treasure the lessons you taught me. I will carry them with me all the days of my life. I am so proud to be your child.

May God watch over you and bless you, with gentleness and with love. As you blessed me. Rest in peace. Amen.

—Rabbi Naomi Levy

PART 4

A Year of Mourning

INTRODUCTION

Upon completing a year of mourning, the four seasons have come and gone. A year may pass too quickly for some or too slowly for others. Though time is passing, it may feel as though it stands still.

Certainly, the Jewish perspective does not presume that an individual will "get over" grieving after a year. One truly is never the same after a loss of a loved one. However, our religion is for the living, and thus, Judaism encourages integrating the loss and grief and reengaging with the world. As life goes on, joy replaces sorrow. Your loved one will always be a part of your life, but their role has now changed. As you accept the finality of death, the grieving process leads you to revisiting life goals and plans, changing perspectives and behavior, and reentering life again.

A Prayer

Help me, God, to listen with my entire being.
When I am in pain, give me the courage to
trust others enough to bare my heart to them.
And when there is no one who will listen, hear
me, God. Hear me and heal me.
Amen.

—Rabbi Naomi Levy, *To Begin Again:*
The Journey Toward Comfort, Strength,
and Faith in Difficult Times, 1998

Dale Norma Oller, MD

Matzevah: The Headstone

Sometime after the end of shloshim (the first thirty days of mourning), I received information from my synagogue regarding the choice of a headstone. In my experience, this was a startlingly early time to ask me for this decision so soon after Earl's death. However, as you likely may discover, the process of having the rabbis agree to its accuracy and appropriateness, combined with the actual engraving of the stone, takes many months. You choose both a stone and also the words to be written in stone. It is a surreal, emotional experience. As the unveiling ceremony approaches, you might prepare to revisit those same emotions you had at the time of death or you might be at a very different emotional place.

It is a mitzvah to erect a memorial marker. Simplicity and dignity are encouraged as they are in all parts of the Jewish tradition surrounding death.

The Unveiling

Dedicating this marker is done through the unveiling ceremony. The unveiling is considered praiseworthy of the family, but it is not required in Jewish tradition. If you choose this ceremony,

People do not die for us immediately, but remain bathed in a sort of aura of life which bears no relation to true immortality but through which they continue to occupy our thoughts as when they were alive. It is as though they were traveling abroad.

—Marcel Proust,
Remembrance of Things Past

Dale Norma Oller, MD

it can be done any time after shloshim and before the first yahrzeit. Many people in my community choose to conduct the unveiling ceremony around the eleventh month. This would not be the case in Israel, where communities tend to unveil just after shloshim.

Some fear that the unveiling will open old wounds. In contrast, for me, there was a powerful, positive psychological aspect to this ceremony. It was yet another "marker" (literal and symbolic). It was a time for me to preview the end of the mourning period.

As I prepared for the unveiling of Earl's stone, I was struck by a number of circumstances that may indeed be something others may resonate with. The time surrounding the death and the funeral is filled with making plans and arrangements, visiting with shiva callers, writing thank you notes for contributions, and attending morning minyan. In direct contrast to the funeral, the unveiling was quieter, less hectic, contemplative, and more reflective.

Personally, I found the weeks before the unveiling a very melancholic time. The reality set in that my husband truly had died. As the unveiling date gets closer, don't be surprised if you have physical symptoms. These symptoms may range from

When My Father Died

I didn't realize that it would be such a physical thing. A death...especially the sudden death of a loved one...is a violent act on our body. I felt very much as if I'd been hit by a plank around the shoulders and the chest. My head felt heavy. It was a stunning experience...I felt like someone stole him from me in the middle of the night...There's such a compelling wish in all of us to be reunited with the people we love. It's so unfathomable when people you love aren't here anymore.

—Marlo Thomas, about the
death of her father, Danny Thomas

fatigue, changes in sleep and appetite, difficulty with concentration and focus, irritability, anxiety, and sensitivity. The brain-body connection is powerful.

Prior to the unveiling, I took the liberty to create a nontraditional ritual at Earl's gravesite. In lieu of bringing cut flowers to a cemetery, Jews mark a visit with a stone. However, Earl's love of roses was compelling. Therefore, I invited his family and close friends to transplant some of his rose bushes to his gravesite.

The unveiling ceremony can be private or open to friends and extended family. It can be officiated by a rabbi or by the family. It is an individual choice. The rabbis have a lovely book of prayers for this brief service. It may be a time for sharing sweet stories of the deceased. It may be a time for renewed tears. It may cause anticipatory sadness that the year of mourning is coming to a close.

As the unveiling was about to begin, I had an odd thought. I remember thinking that I did not want this ceremony to end. It was a once in a lifetime ritual. Then seeing the words I had chosen many months earlier cut in stone was not only powerful but also final. We all used this opportunity to talk again about Earl. When the unveiling ceremony was over, I used the glass from the

A Memorial Prayer

I haven't forgotten you, even though it's been some time now since I've seen your face, touched your hand, heard your voice. You are with me all the time.

I used to think you left me. I know better now. You come to me. Sometimes in the fleeting moments I feel your presence close by. But I still miss you. And nothing, no person, no joy, no accomplishment, no distraction, not even God, can fill the gaping hole your absence has left in my life.

But mixed together with all my sadness, there is a great joy for having known you. I want to thank you for the time we shared, for the love you gave, for the wisdom you spread.

Thank you for the magnificent moments and for the ordinary ones too. There was beauty in our simplicity. Holiness in our unspectacular days. And I will carry the lessons you taught me always.

Your life has ended, but your light can never be extinguished. It continues to shine upon me even on the darkest nights and illuminates my way.

I light this candle in your honor and in your memory. May God bless you as you have blessed me with love, with grace, and with peace. Amen.

—Rabbi Naomi Levy, *Talking to God*, 2002

seven-day memorial candle and made it into a vase to hold Earl's favorite flowers (roses!) for our gathering at home afterwards.

The First Yahrzeit

Yahrzeit is a German word meaning "the time of year." It is observed on the anniversary of the death, not the date of the funeral. It is a mitzvah to observe the anniversary of the day of death by saying the Mourner's Kaddish in synagogue and by lighting a yahrzeit candle in the home. The candle is lit at sundown on the anniversary of the Hebrew date of death. It will burn for twenty-four hours.

Reciting the Mourner's Kaddish may be a combination of: 1) honoring your loved one, 2) renewing a commitment to Judaism, and/or 3) a spiritual opportunity. As you stand to recite the words, you may be acutely aware of your role as a mourner. Therefore, saying the last Mourner's Kaddish at the end of your mourning period might feel like another poignant loss…the loss of your identity as a mourner. Waiting an entire year to stand again to say the Mourner's Kaddish seemed eternal for me.

Both the unveiling and the first yahrzeit observances may bring back waves of sadness. You may not even want those waves to stop. You have sur-

vived a year of experiencing the emotional, physical, and psychological impact of grief. For some, this renewed melancholy might be frightening, but I would suggest it is a normal response, as are all anniversaries of important dates.

As the end of the mourning period approaches, many mourners get mixed messages from those around them. The message may encourage "a time to move back into life" or "a time you should be back to normal." However, these well–meaning messages may not coincide with the tempo of your mourning process.

As Americans, we may also be reminded of the Gregorian calendar date of the death. How to mark that date can be as individual as each death. You may choose to spend the day doing an activity your loved one enjoyed, such as a journey to nature, planting a tree, or gathering with friends and family.

The first yahrzeit can also lead to gratitude for the time you had with your loved one. It might also promote gratitude for those in our lives with whom we now want to nurture relationships…the living. Awareness that over the last year there has been a shift in the family dynamics is often helpful. This is sometimes overlooked after a death. It is frequently underappreciated that family roles

One doesn't know another's sorrow.

—Yiddish proverb

Dale Norma Oller, MD

reorganize. The new balance of the family system may take time and adjustment. It will never be the same again.

Aliyah and Tzedakah

A ritual little known to our community is an opportunity to be called to the Torah at a morning minyan around the yahrzeit date to accept an aliyah. This is the honor of being called upon to read the blessings before and after the Torah reading. Being part of the Torah service is a more concrete acknowledgement than simply remembering the date. Torah reading takes place on Monday, Thursday, and Saturday mornings. This could be a meaningful opportunity for you, even if your Hebrew skills are minimal and/or you have never accepted an aliyah before.

Another traditional ritual is to give tzedakah at the time of the yahrzeit, just as one does during shloshim. The concept is that your loved one can no longer give tzedakah, so we must do this for them and in memory of them.

Upon Completing a Period of Mourning: An Immersion Ceremony

Intention: Kavanah
(To be read before preparing for immersion)

I come here today to mark the end of aveilut, my time of mourning.
Now, as I stand here ready to immerse in mayyim hayyim, living waters,
I prepare to move beyond the formal mourning period, into life with _____ .

Immersion: T'Vilah
First Immersion

(Slowly descend the steps into the mikvah waters, and immerse completely so that every part of your body is covered with water. When you emerge, recite the following blessing:)

Baruch atah, Adonai Elaheinhu, Melech ha'olam Asher kidshanu bi-t'vilah b'mayyim hayyim.

Blessed are You, God, Majestic Spirit of the Universe who makes us holy by embracing us in living waters.

Second Immersion
(To be read before you immerse)

To everything there is a season, A time to be born, a time to die,

The Mikvah

Over the last few decades, the use of the mikvah in nontraditional ways has grown across our country. One of these ways is to use it to mark the completion of the mourning period. Just as the mikvah is filled with living waters, the ritual of immersion in the mikvah to mark the end of the mourning period promises transition into a time to engage with those in your life who are living.

The ceremony shared in this book may be meaningful for you. In Portland, a lovely new facility called Rachel's Well is welcoming and soothing.

Personally, I have found the use of the mikvah a very spiritual activity. For a number of years, I have marked the month of Elul in preparation for the High Holidays with a mikvah ceremony specifically written for the new year by a group in the Boston area named Mayyim Hayyim, meaning "Living Waters." Similarly, this group has provided the ceremony shown on the adjacent page of this book and gives permission to copy and share it. They also have a ceremony of immersion prayers for the completion of shloshim.

A time to weep, a time to laugh.

As I have been in a time of mourning, now may I move into a time of healing.
(Take a deep breath and exhale completely, while gently and completely immersing for a second time.)

Third Immersion
(To be read before you immerse)

Time flows through us like water.
The past and the dead speak through us.
Blessed is the memory of the one whose life touched mine. May ____'s memory be a blessing.
(Relax and let your body soften, as you slowly and completely immerse for the third time.)

Fourth Immersion
(Take a moment for personal reflection)

(Take a deep breath, exhale completely, and immerse for the fourth time.

When you emerge, recite the following:)

I emerge from these living waters, strengthened to move forward into the fullness of life. As the Torah says: I have put before you life and death... (Therefore) choose life.

Acceptance

Elisabeth Kübler-Ross, a 1960s pioneer in talking openly about dying and death, wrote of the five stages of grieving. While this concept has been questioned and revised, her description of the stage of "acceptance" is hard to dispute. The role acceptance plays in helping a mourner move on in life is consistent with Judaism's ritual practices. This word, "acceptance," is not an easy one to "accept." It can be very gradual and associated with intermittently easier or more difficult times. Acceptance can lead to finding a "new normal," which may include feeling functional, creative, and happy. While you never forget your loved one, life does go on. Comfort comes from thinking that your loved one would wish you joy, happiness, and connection to the world again.

Grief entails learning to live with reminders of the deceased loved one, reconnecting with others, understanding and recognizing painful emotions, and thinking about finding meaning and moving into the future.

David Kessler, a world-famous grief expert, shared how he found meaning after the sudden death of his twenty-one-year-old son in his book titled *Finding Meaning: The Sixth Stage of Grief.*

"Meaning comes through finding a way to sustain your love for the person after their death while you're moving forward with your life. Loss is simply what happens to you in life. Meaning is what *you* make happen."

Finding meaning doesn't eliminate grief, a sense of loss, or need for bereavement. It simply is about finding meaning. It can take many possible forms. I believe I found meaning after my husband's death by writing this book and later publishing it to share with others.

This is not to say grief is something one "gets over." Phyllis Silverman studied grief and bereavement much of her life. At the age of eighty-eight, she was in hospice care while her final work was accepted for publication. She helped us to see bereavement as not only a process that never ends but one that shapes life. Finding your own personal strategies and coping mechanisms to care for your vulnerabilities is of utmost importance during this time.

A Prayer for the Power to Return from the Depths of Sorrow

Teach me always to believe in my power to return to life, to hope, and to You, God, no matter what pains I have endured, no matter how far I have strayed from You. Give me the strength to resurrect my weary spirit. Revive me, God, so I can embrace life once more in joy, in passion, in peace. Amen.

—Rabbi Naomi Levy, *Talking to God*, 2002

Prolonged Grief

Grief and bereavement are universal. Barbara Roberts, former Oregon governor, offers some wonderful, honest, and sound advice in her book, *Death Without Denial, Grief Without Apology: A Guide for Facing Death and Loss*. Following the death of her husband, Frank Roberts, she wrote: "Grief is hard to bear. It feels as if you will never be whole again. The permanence of death and the finality of the loss can leave you feeling as if you can never be happy again. And to some degree that is true. You will never be able to share happy times again with the deceased person you love. The memories, pictures, and perhaps some belongings are all you have left. And for a long time, these memories and mementos may bring you more pain than comfort…But while grief is a difficult experience, there is much to be learned from those who have been through the work of grieving, facing the pain and finally learning to live again."

It would seem perfectly "normal" after the mourning year is complete to continue to have yearning, longing, and preoccupation with your loved one, sorrow and pain from the death, and an excessive focus with the circumstances around the death. Judaism understands this and therefore encourages moving into the world of the living.

PART 5

Afterword

Covid-19 Virtual Mourning

Parts of this book were written during the COVID-19 pandemic. Much has been written about historic pandemics, such as Albert Camus' *The Plague*, Mary Shelley's *The Last Man*, Jack London's *The Scarlet Plague*, and Edgar Allan Poe's *The Masque of the Red Death*. I personally am drawn to the sound of Gabriel Garcia Marquez's *Love In The Time of Cholera*.

Deaths, funerals, shiva minyanim, saying the Mourner's Kaddish, and "Mourning in the Time of COVID" became rituals observed virtually. Who would have imagined a virtual funeral or shiva minyan? Yet, in compliance with both Judaism's emphasis on "life" and the governor's emphasis on safety by sheltering-in-place, new

*God, grant me the serenity to accept the things
I cannot change, courage to change the things I
can, and the wisdom to know the difference.*

—Reinhold Niebuhr

Dale Norma Oller, MD

and creative and compassionate adjustments were implemented during the pandemic. Zoom, Google Duo Streamlining, and FaceTime became household words.

Two events occurred in my family during the beginning of the pandemic that stand out as memorable. Both happened just before the order came to shelter-in-place, yet we were very aware of the spreading pandemic. First, my young thirty-seven-year-old nephew died suddenly of a massive heart attack. It may have been the last "real"/non-virtual funeral of my congregation before such gatherings were deemed too dangerous for health and safety. The abrupt shock and young age of my nephew's death was an example of how important presence, touch, and sincere compassion are woven into rituals. Jewish funerals are never a matter of being invited. It is a "mitzvah" and obligation to be present to support the mourners. We all sobbed and hugged, sharing tears together at such a sad loss of such a wonderful young man.

That same week was the second memorable family event. It was the fourth anniversary of my husband's death date on the Jewish calendar. It marks the yearly time that the family says the Mourner's Kaddish, the prayer remember-

The Jewish mourning cycle allows for a phased recovery from loss. In fact, this cycle continues throughout the life of the mourner through the vehicles of Yizkor and Yahrzeit. Judaism, however, is a religion focused on the living, not on the deceased. Thus, Jewish tradition cautions the mourner against excessive grief.

—Dr. Ron Wolfson

ing the individual who has died. Normally, the family attends services at the synagogue, where the names of those remembered are read. In the presence of the congregation and with the required ten to make a minyan, the family stands to say the Mourner's Kaddish. Yet this was the first Shabbat my synagogue began streamlining, in lieu of gathering for services. We were nine around the table. We creatively identified the electronic streamlining machine as our tenth to make a minyan for us to say the Mourner's Kaddish. My son was the first to stand. The four grandchildren, eyes as big as saucers, watching and following our lead stood and we all joined the Rabbi in a Virtual Mourner's Kaddish prayer.

"Mourning in the Time of COVID" has taken on new meaning. Kessler, a grief expert, reminds us that finding meaning is the sixth stage of grief.

Linda Magistris of The Good Grief Trust describes grieving during a pandemic. She discusses dying alone in hospital quarantines, virtual funerals, no touch, no hand-holding or giving a hug to the mourners, and everyone isolating and sheltering in place. The basic principle of attending to mourners is presence. That has been prohibited during the pandemic, COVID-19. It turns upside-down all of the helpful rituals Judaism had

provided. However, we are an adaptable group and value LIFE above all.

Jewish references to the first "quarantine" often point to Noah's Flood (or plague). A mixed message from our Biblical stories of plagues are that they are a result of sin and God's punishment. Yet, the symbol in Noah's story is of the dove carrying an olive branch, which represents HOPE.

Virtual mourning of loss during the COVID pandemic, where funerals are often private, limited to ten people, and shiva minyanim are Zoomed, creates a mixed response. The threat of the catastrophic virus is real. The psychological conflict between human closeness and safe distance is ever-present. Grieving in 2020 can be very lonely for mourners sheltered in place, without touch or physical closeness. Yet virtual gatherings can include relatives and friends from anywhere in the world. This can bring solace and meaning to many mourners. Community presence is an important value in Jewish ritual.

Rabbi David Kosak, senior rabbi of Congregation Neveh Shalom in Portland, Oregon, states: "For me, shiva minyanim are one of the rituals that has translated most effectively to an online format. True, we can't offer one another hugs, and we can't feel the palpable sense of another's

presence. Nonetheless, something real is created. We are able to let a mourner sense that they are not alone, and providing a space in which to share stories about a loved one remains both available and deeply healing."

The sequelae of the COVID-19 pandemic and mourning through virtual rituals is yet to be fully appreciated. Some believe we will measure the mental health toll through suicide rates. The rates have not increased in the early months of the pandemic, but may with time.

The sequelae may be attributed to the serious issues of unnatural isolation and loneliness. It may be attributed to uncertainty of the future and economic insecurity. It may be attributed to being overwhelmed by the huge numbers of deaths and gruesome scenes from hospitals. It may be attributed to anticipatory grief about potential loss of a loved one or about safety and control of life during a pandemic.

Anticipatory grief may appear as anxiety symptoms, associated with fears of the unknown. Anticipatory grief may appear as depressive symptoms, associated with loss of friends, family, and the thousands we hear and read about. Anxiety and depression are not the same as grieving, per se, although there are many overlapping symptoms.

A Prayer When a Loved One Dies by Suicide

Why, God? Why did he have to take his life? Why couldn't I help him? Why couldn't he hold on? Why didn't You save him? Why?

How, God? How will I recover from this nightmare? How can I exorcise the guilt: "I could have done more," "I should have done more," "If only I had..." How do I forgive myself? How do I forgive him?

Help me, God. Give me strength to carry on. Heal my anger and shame. Ease the burden on my heart. Teach me to believe that I am not to blame. Lead me back to life and hope and joy.

I know the pain became too much for him. Death was his only hope for release from his suffering. Life offered him no such promise, no relief.

Let him rest now, God. Free from all that haunted him. At peace, at last. Watch over him, God. Be his comfort. Grant him the serenity that he so longed for in life. Let his death be his healing.

Amen.

—Rabbi Naomi Levy

After a Death by Suicide

Finally, a topic that many have a great deal of difficulty discussing...SUICIDE. Grief after a suicide has unique issues. Our culture is uncomfortable talking about death to begin with, and even more uncomfortable talking about suicide. The grief is impacted by the fact that the surrounding support is statistically often less and more isolating after a suicide. We give people who have lost a loved one by suicide less support because of misunderstanding and stigma.

One important topic is our choice of words as we talk about this topic. "Committing suicide," "completed suicide," and "successful suicide" are frequently used phrases. "Committing" is a word used in criminality and has no place in this discussion. As David Kessler states in his lectures, "there is nothing successful about suicide." "Completed suicide" also has no place in our vocabulary as we offer support to the loved ones who are dealing with a death by suicide. The stigma is so strong that some families would rather lie about this death than face their own and others stigma.

Understanding the connection between suicide and impulsivity, the inability to be able to see a hopeful future, and the fact that many who die by

Grief is like living two lives. One is where you "pretend" everything is alright, and the other is where your heart silently screams in pain.

—Unknown

suicide are undiagnosed with mental illness would help this stigmatizing death. Families need more support than ever in this situation.

Historically, death by suicide was also stigmatizing in Judaism. There were times when the bodies of those who died by suicide were placed at the periphery of the cemetery. Thankfully, this is circumvented by today's clergy and new interpretations.

Particularly, as the pandemic of COVID-19 leaves an increase in mental health issues in its wake, we are expecting a rise in suicide rates, above the already rising rates prior to the pandemic.

AFTER A DEATH BY HOMICIDE

A death by homicide is unfathomable and unmentioned in our current writings about grief, bereavement, and mourning from a Jewish perspective.

However, America and the world at-large are now mourning loudly, with a great deal of anger, death by homicide in the Black Lives Matter movement.

National grief, collective grief, and trans-generational grief are being witnessed in 2020. Our Jewish history of the Holocaust knows this grief of death by murder all too well. Today's Jewish rituals

You can't prevent birds of sorrow from flying over your head...but you can prevent them from building nests in your hair.

—Chinese proverb

Dale Norma Oller, MD

of mourning never forget this backdrop. Moving through the journey of grief never forgets the need to move toward LIFE!

Conclusion

This book is intended to: 1) provide basic information about the role of Jewish rituals surrounding death, 2) share how I incorporated these rituals into my own personal experience, and most importantly, 3) offer support.

My hope is that reading this book has brought comfort, empathy, information, compassion, and assistance.

Acknowledgements

I owe a great deal of thanks to Nancy Prouser, Jamie Passaro, and Jennifer McGrath for their hours of editorial help. They helped me think more deeply. They helped me reframe stories to be clear. They were tireless with structural corrections. I appreciate my friend and colleague Marcia Liberson for her heartfelt words in the Foreword. I also thank graphic artist Danielle Lewis for her illustration.

Most importantly, I am also deeply grateful to Earl, my wise husband of forty-six years, who helped prepare me to write this book upon his death. He taught many people how to die with grace and openness. He continually demonstrated his beautiful soul traits.

Selected Bibliography

Akner, Lois; LCSW, *How to Survive the Loss of a Parent*, 1993 (A Guide for Adults).

Angelou, Issokson and Kummer; Mayyim Hayyim Living Waters Community Mikvah; Boston; "Upon Completing a Period of Mourning."

Brener, Rabbi Anne; LCSW; *Taking the Time You Need to Mourn Your Loss*; Life Lights, 2000 (series of Jewish help for wholeness and healing).

Brener, Rabbi Anne; LCSW; *Mourning Mitzvah: A Guided Journal for Walking the Mourner's Path Through Grief to Healing*, 1993/2001.

Brother Toby; Reflection; Starcross Monastic Community, Nov. 2016.

Brody, Jane E.; "Making Meaning Out of Grief," *The New York Times*, Nov. 4, 2019.

Chodron, Pema; *When Things Fall Apart: Heart Advice for Difficult Times*, 2005.

Cowan, Rabbi Rachel; *Coping with the Death of a Spouse*; Life Lights, 2000.

Diamant, Anita; *Saying Kaddish: How to Comfort the Dying, Bury the Dead & Mourn as a Jew*, 1998.

Ericsson, Stephanie; *Companion Through the Darkness*, 1993.

Falk, Marcia; various publications.

Friedman, Rabbi Dayle A.; *Jewish Wisdom for Growing Older*, 2015.

Goldstein, Rabbi Zalman; *The Jewish Mourner's Companion, Guidance. Comfort. Liturgy;* 2006.

Grollman, Dr. Earl A.; *Living When a Loved One Has Died*, 1977.

Grollman, Dr. Earl A.; "Living with your loss," 1991.

Haugk, Kenneth C.; *Journeying Through Grief,* 2004 (series of 4 books used by Stephen Ministries).

Hensley, Paula and Clayton, Paula; Psychiatric Annals 43:6/ June, 2013.

Homer, *The Iliad*, circa 1260-1240 B.C.

Isaak, Rabbi Daniel; *Death & Mourning: A Jewish Guide to Grieving & Comforting the Bereaved;* Congregation Neveh Shalom; Portland, OR.

Kamens, Rabbi Sylvan and Riemer, Rabbi Jack; "We Remember Them," Plaza Jewish Community Chapel, Inc.

Kelman, Rabbi Stuart and Fendel, Dan; *Nihum Aveilim: A Guide for the Comforter*, Gamliel Institute, 2015.

Kessler, David; "Finding Meaning: The Sixth Stage of Grief," 2019.

Kübler-Ross, Elisabeth; *On Death and Dying*, 1969.

Kumar, Sameet M.; *Grieving Mindfully: A Compassionate and Spiritual Guide to Coping with Loss*, 2005 (psychologist at the Memorial Healthcare System Cancer Institute in south Broward, Florida).

Lamm, Rabbi Maurice; *The Jewish Way in Death and Mourning*, 1969.

Levy, Rabbi Naomi; *To Begin Again: The Journey Toward Comfort, Strength, and Faith in Difficult Times*, 1998.

Levy, Rabbi Naomi; *Talking to God: Personal Prayers for Times of Joy, Sadness, Struggle, and Celebration*, 2002

Levy, Rabbi Naomi; *Hope Will Find You: My Search for the Wisdom to Stop Waiting and Start Living*, 2010.

Mandell, Sherri; *The Blessing of a Broken Heart*, 2009 (National Jewish Book Awards winner).

Matlins, Stuart M.; *The Jewish Book of Grief & Healing: A Spiritual Companion for Mourning*; (newly edited book with preface by Rabbi Anne Brener and Foreword by Dr. Ron Wolfson).

McGrath, Tom; *CareNotes for Teens: When Your Grandparent Dies*; Abbey Press Publications, 1999.

McNees, Pat; *Dying: A Book of Comfort, Healing Words on Loss and Grief*, 1996.

Olds, Sharon; *The Dead and the Living*, 1992.

Olitzky, Rabbi Kerry M.; *Grief in Our Seasons: A Mourner's Kaddish Companion* (Jewish Lights Publishing), 2000.

O'Rourke, Meghan; "Good Grief: Is There a Better Way to Be Bereaved?"; *The New Yorker*, February 1, 2010.

Psychiatric Annals, Bereavement, Depression and the DSM-5, June 2013 (Academic Journal).

Reynolds, Charles. F. III, et al; *Diagnosis and Treatment of Complicated Grief*, UPMC, 2011.

Roberts, Barbara K.; *Death Without Denial; Grief Without Apology*, 2002 (Former Oregon governor's guide for facing death and loss).

Schrag, Mort; *Recovering From Your Child's Suicide*, 2002, (Compassionate Friends of Westside Jewish Community Center, Los Angeles, CA).

Schrag, Mort; *Walking Through the Valley of the Shadow: When a Jewish Child Dies*; 2003.

Shenker, Lois Sussman; *A Blessed Dying*, 2011.

Silverman, Phyllis R.; *Widow to Widow: How the Bereaved Help One Another*, 2004.

Winant, Katey Geyer; *One Washcloth, One Towel*, 2011 (short piece of wisdom after the death of a spouse).

Wolfson, Dr. Ron; *From Death Through Shiva: A Guide to Jewish Grieving Practices*; Life Lights, 2000 (series of Jewish help for wholeness and healing).

Wolfson, Dr. Ron; *A Time to Mourn, a Time to Comfort*, Jewish Lights Publishing, 2005.

About the Author

Dale Norma Oller, MD, has practiced psychiatry in Portland, Oregon, for thirty years, specializing in women's psychiatric issues. After her husband, Earl, died in 2016, Oller wrote this book about her bereavement, integrating quotes, wisdom, and the experiences of others on their journeys of grief. She expresses gratitude for the rabbinic guidance at Congregation Neveh Shalom, for the stories of grief that her patients have shared through the years, and for the voices of the women in her widows group.

Made in the USA
Monee, IL
06 October 2020